FOUNDATIONS

SHAPING THE MINISTRY
OF CHRISTIAN EDUCATION
IN YOUR CONGREGATION

D1379225

DISCIPLESHIP RESOURCES

MATERIALS FOR GROWTH IN CHRISTIAN FAITH & LIFE

— NASHVILLE, TENNESSEE —

❖ **TO PLACE AN ORDER** OR TO INQUIRE ABOUT RESOURCES AND CUSTOMER ACCOUNTS, CONTACT:

DISCIPLESHIP RESOURCES DISTRIBUTION CENTER
P.O. BOX 6996
ALPHARETTA, GEORGIA 30239-6996

TEL: (800) 685-4370

FAX: (404) 442-5114

❖ ❖ ❖

❖ **FOR EDITORIAL INQUIRIES** AND RIGHTS AND PERMISSIONS REQUESTS, CONTACT:

DISCIPLESHIP RESOURCES EDITORIAL OFFICES
P.O. BOX 840
NASHVILLE, TENNESSEE 37202-0840

TEL: (615) 340-7068

Cover design by Tim Hornbeak.

Library of Congress Catalog Card No. 93-71103

ISBN 0-88177-123-6

Unless otherwise indicated, all scripture quotations are taken from the New Revised Standard Version of the Holy Bible, © 1989 by the Division of Christian Education of the National Council of Churches of Christ in the USA and used by permission.

DR123

✞ CONTENTS

✝ Preface

The Book of Discipline 1992, charges the General Board of Discipleship with the responsibility for developing "... a clear statement of the biblical and theological foundations of Christian education, consistent with the doctrines of The United Methodist Church and the purpose of the board" (Par. 1207.1). Additionally, the General Board has responsibility for "formulating and interpreting the educational philosophy and approach which shall undergird and give coherence to all the educational work of the Church ..." (Par. 1208.1). The General Board of Discipleship, through the Curriculum Resources Committee is responsible for developing "... curriculum and curriculum resources ... consistent with the educational philosophy and approach formulated for the educational ministry of the Church by the General Board of Discipleship and shall reflect a unity of purpose and a planned comprehensiveness of scope" (Par. 1224.3). And every congregation has the following charge: "In each local church there shall be a church school for the purpose of accomplishing the church's educational ministry in accordance with Paragraph 1208" (Par. 264.1).

In 1988 delegates to General Conference adopted "Our Theological Task" which appears in *The Book of Discipline, 1992*, Paragraph 68, Section 4. With a new statement of the theological task of The United Methodist Church, the Christian education staff of the General Board of Discipleship saw the need to bring to the church a new statement of the biblical and theological foundations of Christian education. Following the 1988 General Conference, the General Board of Discipleship appointed a task force to begin the process of developing the foundational statement for Christian education. This task force included representatives from local church education, theological schools, board members of the Section on Christian Education and the Curriculum Resources Committee of the General Board of Discipleship, and staff members from the Section on Christian Education and Church School

Publications. The task force included regional representation and cultural/racial constituencies. The task force began meeting in 1989, gathering data, accumulating information, and writing drafts of material to be included in a final document.

In 1992, staff members from the Section on Christian Education and Church School Publications of the General Board of Discipleship took the work of the task force and produced the document, *Foundations: Shaping the Ministry of Christian Education in Your Congregation.* In February 1993 the General Board of Discipleship approved this document and gave to staff the responsibility to complete and publish the manuscript for use by all congregations in shaping their various educational ministries.

Foundations: Shaping the Ministry of Christian Education in Your Congregation hopes to articulate the purpose of and provide support for all educational ministries in The United Methodist Church. We commend this resource to you in building your ministry of Christian education.

Christian Education Staff
General Board of Discipleship
May 1993

✝ Introduction

When the Nortons' first child was to be baptized, they planned a party. This party, like the ceremony at church, marked for Benjamin and his parents the beginning of his faith journey. Of course it had a beginning point prior to his baptism, but at his baptism his mother and father would be standing, with the support of their congregation and their families, pledging to guide, to teach, to love, to care for him in the Christian faith. With tears, laughter, joy, and hope they presented him to their pastors for that outward sign of God's grace and God's claim on Benjamin. Afterwards they celebrated the beginning of Benjamin's faith journey with friends and relatives. They celebrated the support of family and congregational members. They celebrated the love of God which surrounds each person. And the next day they wondered, "Now what?"

Each of us who has brought a child to be baptized has asked the same questions: "What should I teach her?" "What am I learning from him?" "Am I doing all I can do to surround this person with knowledge upon which to build faith, with experiences upon which to center faith, with the love and care out of which faith can grow?" And as we ask ourselves these questions, we also ask the same questions of our church. What is the church's plan for helping us grow in faith, not only when we are children but throughout our entire lives? It is not a simple question. It is one filled with passion and fear and anxiety and wonder. We want our church to have a plan for our children's journeys into faith. We also want that as adults. And we want it for every child, every youth, and every adult in our congregation. We want a plan that takes seriously our beliefs in God, that proclaims God's promises to us, and that takes seriously our promises to God and to the community to lead a life of faith, of good works, of reverence for all of creation. How does our congregation make plans for continually passing on the faith to all who seek to know God?

Foundations: Shaping the Ministry of Christian Education in Your Congregation forms the beginning of your plan for teaching and learning. It will not be the whole of your plan. Instead it will be a starting place. Read these images of "starting places" and think of your own congregation:

◆ For an artist, the foundation is that first splash of color onto the bare canvas. Its placement and brilliance will influence the way the picture unfolds.

◆ For a quilter, the foundation is the center piece of the quilt. The pattern of the center pieces will be reflected in the entire quilt, radiating out from the center.

◆ For a builder, the foundation is that upon which the entire structure will rest. Whether wood or concrete, the base must be carefully crafted to hold the structure which rises from this start.

The starting place determines the pattern of the whole. To be strong, to be in harmony, to be whole means beginning with a foundation that is not happenstance, but planned; not impulsive, but intentional; not random, but created with each part in careful relationship with the other. Chapters 1-6 feature questions for discussion/contemplation to help you begin looking at specific ways to apply *Foundations* to the life and work of your congregation and community. Extra space is provided at the end of each chapter for notetaking.

The starting place offered in *Foundations: Shaping the Ministry of Christian Education in Your Congregation* encourages you to do the following:

◆ See teaching as a fundamental ministry of the community of faith as well as a series of programs;

◆ Pay more attention to the ways you teach even as you pay attention to what you teach;

◆ Live out your vision for teaching and learning in local congregations, with annual conferences and general church agencies giving support and encouragement;

◆ Emphasize teaching and learning for the community of faith as much as you emphasize it for individuals;

◆ Understand teaching as transformation as well as transmission of the stories, language, and symbols of faith;

◆ Take who you teach, how they learn, and where they learn as seriously as you take content;

◆ Seek teachers with a growing and maturing faith as eagerly as you seek quality curriculum resources;

◆ Create new and different settings for learning at the same time that you strengthen traditional church schools;

◆ Integrate Christian education into the total life of the congregation, as well as see it as a unique ministry of the congregation.

With this as your starting point, it is now time to begin painting a picture, constructing a building, sewing a quilt of Christian education in your congregation for the twenty-first century.

Chapter 1
Foundations for the Ministry of Christian Education in The United Methodist Church

The church of Jesus Christ cannot survive without the fundamental ministry of teaching. During his life, Jesus was known and loved first of all as Rabbi or teacher. His teachings were compelling, and his followers eagerly waited to hear what he would say next. They were known as *disciples*, which means "learners." Every time we call ourselves and others Christian disciples, we remember that we are the ones who are learning the faith given to us by our teacher, Jesus. Matthew's Gospel tells of Jesus challenging his followers to continue his teaching ministry:

> *Go therefore and make disciples of all nations, baptizing them in the name of the Father and of the Son and of the Holy Spirit, and teaching them to obey everything that I have commanded you (Matthew 28:19-20).*

The church of Jesus Christ is called to teach! Jesus' commandment gives to all disciples both the responsibility and the authority to teach as Jesus taught. The church of Jesus Christ cannot fully be the church without the fundamental ministry of teaching. Members of the congregation must have opportunities to learn the faith and to explore ways of living what they have learned every day. The United Methodist Church and its predecessor bodies

Write about an influential teacher you have had, either now or earlier in your life. What about that teacher made an impression upon you?

What do you want to happen in your church because of its educational ministry?

have given us a rich educational tradition. Since the very beginning, that tradition has included Sunday school and through-the-week educational offerings for all ages. The ministry of teaching is and always has been essential to the very life of the congregation.

Foundations: Shaping the Ministry of Christian Education in Your Congregation provides the foundation for effective ministries of Christian education in United Methodist congregations. It is written especially to encourage dialogue and to assist planning in local congregations. They provide the primary place where the essential ministry of the Christian education of the people of God happens. But above all, *Foundations* is essential reading for all those who give leadership to that ministry in and through congregations.

Every creation must begin with a solid foundation. A painter must begin with high quality canvas and paints if her work of art is to last for generations. When building a house, the contractor uses the best materials possible, measures carefully, chooses the best workers. Starting with poor materials, sloppy measurements, and workers who do not know what they are doing results in a weak and shoddy structure. This book offers a foundation from which to create the ministry of Christian education in your congregation. The components of that foundation include **describing the task** of those responsible for Christian education in the congregation, **understanding the purpose** of that ministry, and **faithfully affirming** what a congregation teaches through its ministry of Christian education. This foundation provides the essential starting point so that the task of building a strong and vital educational ministry can go forward. This chapter sets forth foundational statements about our task, and the remaining chapters expand on those statements.

Foundations has two primary purposes. The first is to provide foundations from which congregations can create strong ministries of Christian education. The second is to invite congregations to begin an ongoing process of shaping that ministry for the twenty-first century. This shaping process will continually strengthen the foundation and, therefore, result in new and ever-stronger ministries of Christian education. That can happen only when a continuing dialogue takes place among all persons involved. When their planning process includes a free-flowing dialogue, they will discover that their ability to generate insights and ideas as a group is greater than the ability of any one member of the group thinking alone.

DESCRIBING THE TASK

The congregation's leaders in Christian education are responsible for the systematic and intentional effort to create, support, and provide resources for settings in which the ministry of teaching takes place.

Every congregation chooses leaders to be responsible for the ministry of Christian education. In The United Methodist Church, this includes persons named to the work area on Christian education, the nurture chairperson, Sunday school superintendent, the pastor, and other staff. Strong pastoral and lay leadership will enable these leaders to create the most effective ministry of Christian education possible. Among other things, these leaders determine the most effective time for teaching and learning to take place. The example in the following paragraph tells how one congregation learned the importance of these decisions.

A neighborhood congregation in the suburbs of a large city asks each member who joins the church to make a two-hour commitment on Sunday mornings.

Who are the leaders in Christian education in your congregation? Can you name leaders other than those who hold specific offices?

That commitment includes both worship and Sunday school. However, at one time the church had two worship services, with Sunday school following the second service. That schedule made it impossible for those who chose the early service to meet their goal of a two-hour commitment. So the Christian education leaders worked with those planning worship to revise the schedule and to have Sunday school between the two worship services. Before long, a group of adults who attended the early service asked to start an "Earlybirds" class before worship. A few months later, the planning group came up with the idea of serving a light lunch after the second service for a group of single young adults. Both of those alternative classes included members who had never attended Sunday school.

In defining the task, it is important to understand the boundaries of the task as well. Those responsible for the ministry of Christian education are not also responsible for the total teaching ministry of the church. The teaching ministry belongs to *all* the people and it must not be isolated from other forms of ministry. In a real sense, every person in the congregation participates in the teaching ministry. We teach through worship, through service, through engagement in the administrative tasks of the church. Everyone in the congregation is both teacher and learner. Thomas Langford states it well:

> To teach is to contribute to the total formation of Christian life; teaching is done by deed and action as well as by word. And what is taught is not doctrine in an abstract way but "practical divinity." That is, doctrine undergirding and enriching Christian existence. . . . The goal of teaching in Methodism is not uniquely focused on rational consensus in doctrinal construction. The aim is holistic. We teach in order to provide authentic worship and service; teaching is for the sculpting of life. The means of teaching are

totalistic: teaching is a part of every activity and is effective if it conveys ways of living.[1]

Langford makes it clear that the ministry of teaching and learning happens in many formal and informal settings that may be outside the boundary of traditional Christian education. The specific task of the congregation's leaders in Christian education is to create, support, and provide resources for settings in which the fundamental ministry of teaching will take place. This ministry of Christian education is essential to the life of the congregation.

UNDERSTANDING THE PURPOSE

Through Christian education we invite people and communities of faith to be transformed as they are inspired and challenged to:

- **Know and experience God through Jesus Christ,**
- **Claim and live God's promises, and**
- **Grow and serve as Christian disciples.**

Imagine that this statement of purpose is a tapestry. The weaver has in mind a pattern to be woven and gathers all the many colors of yarn that will be needed. She then weaves the threads together to form the pattern. She does not use the colors in sequential order, using all of the red before any of the blue. Instead she combines the threads to create a beautiful and elaborate picture that can be seen only as the weaving progresses. In the same way, we do not first teach what it means to know and experience God and, only when we are assured that has been accomplished, move on to teach what it means to claim and live God's promises. We accomplish our purpose when we continually weave together all of the elements. The threads appear and disappear, forming a beautiful tapestry that represents the faith of diverse persons and communities. As the pattern

Study this purpose statement carefully. Throughout your reading and reflecting, make notes about the ways in which this purpose is lived out in your congregation. Also make notes about how you would change this purpose statement to make it more your own.

emerges, we see the wholeness God intends for each person, for the community of believers, and for all creation. We realize that, while we can create the settings and provide and support teachers for those settings, the transformation of persons is beyond our doing. God is the weaver of the tapestry. It is God who, through grace, works the miracle of transformation. We are servants of the one who does the weaving.

Weaving done without a pattern may result in a tapestry that is neither beautiful nor useful. Seeking to shape a ministry of Christian education without a pattern or purpose can lead us to engage in activities unrelated to the desired outcome. Understanding our purpose provides the pattern which is essential to the building of a strong ministry. The dominant thread that establishes and defines the pattern is the thread of God's grace. That thread will be woven throughout the following chapters, for the ministry of Christian education is inextricably bound together with God's miracle of grace.

Chapter 2 will focus on the overall purpose of transformation through challenge and engagement. Chapter 3 will explore what it means to know and experience God through Jesus Christ. Chapter 4 focuses on one understanding of faith as "trusting the promises of God" and describes that trust as claiming and living those promises. Chapter 5 explores the meaning of growing and serving as Christian disciples. Chapter 6 looks at the statement as the foundation from which to create an effective ministry of Christian education.

Affirming Our Ministry

We believe in God, revealed through Jesus Christ, the Holy Spirit, and creation, as witnessed to through the scripture, the worship, and the traditions of the faith, and we affirm that all of us, through our participation in Christian education, will:

◆ Declare that God is present and active in the world;

◆ Know the content of the Bible and the Christian faith;

◆ Reflect on, discuss, witness to, and live our faith;

◆ Make decisions based on our Christian values;

◆ Discern and respond to the ministry to which God calls us;

◆ Grow in God's grace and in the gifts God has given us for ministry;

◆ Engage in a lifelong journey of learning and living the faith.

How has the educational ministry of your church dealt with these affirmations during the past quarter? Have some affirmations received more attention than others? If so, why?

What changes would you make in these affirmations?

When Christian education settings and the teachers who teach in them are shaped by these affirmations, lives will be transformed by the power of God's grace. Persons will come to know and experience God through Jesus Christ, to claim and live God's promises, and they will grow and serve as Christian disciples.

We need to carefully design the settings through which our ministry of Christian education takes place so that we will achieve our purpose. And then we need to be equally as careful about what is taught within those settings. The purpose of Christian education and the goal of our teaching ministry are one and the same: the transformation of persons and communities. Thus, every teacher in every setting needs to know and to be committed to that overarching purpose.

THE MINISTRY OF CHRISTIAN EDUCATION AND THE PRIMARY TASK OF THE CONGREGATION

The primary task of every congregation is to reach out to people where they are and to receive them as they are, to relate them to God through Jesus Christ, to nurture their growth in faith, and to

How does your congregation carry out this primary task through its Christian education?

send them into the world to live as disciples of Jesus Christ. Our ministry of Christian education is important to the accomplishment of every part of this primary task. Christian education settings can be entry points for persons into the congregation, places to reach out and receive others. Persons come to know God and make life-changing decisions in those settings, whether they are toddlers in the two-year-old class or the oldest adult in a weekly Bible study session. They are encouraged to grow and mature in the faith and are sent forth as Christian disciples to make the world more loving and just.

Christian education is a fundamental ministry through which the whole of the primary task is accomplished. It provides the primary place of nurture in the faith for most people in congregations, the place where they learn the content of the faith and explore ways to live their faith day by day. And so our ministry of Christian education is interwoven with the primary task of the congregation and is essential to the fulfillment of that task.

[1]Thomas A. Langford in *By What Authority*, Elizabeth Box Price and Charles R. Foster, eds. (Nashville: Abingdon, 1991), p. 65.

 NOTES

CHAPTER 2
INVITE PEOPLE TO BE TRANSFORMED

The young woman sits at the potter's wheel with a formless lump of clay. She places it on the wheel and, as the wheel begins to spin, she touches the clay with skillful hands. She knows that the clay has unique qualities — color, texture, weight — all of which can make it a thing of beauty. As she pays attention to those qualities and spins the wheel, the clay seems to come alive and, under her hands, the lump begins to take shape. As the wheel turns, a beautiful and useful pitcher begins to emerge. The potter smiles as she sees her vision and the qualities of the clay combine. The clay is being transformed, changed, by a combination of its unique qualities, her skillful hands, and the magic of her potter's wheel.

Through our ministry of Christian education we invite persons and communities of faith to be transformed by God's grace much as that lump of clay was transformed. Transformation is a continual process of being converted or changed so that our fullest humanity can be realized. It might begin in a single moment, like a raging flood that radically alters the lay of the land. Or it might be a slow process, like water seeping through the earth, gradually creating new paths and patterns within the land. In both cases it is God's grace that does the transforming work. Our task is to provide numerous and diverse settings

Where do you see individuals and the community of faith being transformed by God? Can you name people, times, and events in which transformation occurred?

Pat Lombardo

and creative teaching which will inspire and challenge persons to open themselves to the possibility of God's transforming grace. The hope that sustains us in that task is the vision of persons and communities living in harmony with the will and way of God.

Christian education settings should be inviting places, and when we teach we should teach invitationally, expecting that lives will be transformed.

> *The Christian church grows because people in the church invite others to join with them in this Christian pilgrimage. The Christian faith is a people-to-people movement. It began with the ministry of Jesus of Nazareth, the calling of the early disciples, and the spread of the movement after Jesus' death and resurrection. The disciples and others who believed that Jesus was the Christ, the Son of God, spread the word. This good news captured the imagination and loyalty of many in that first century setting. And from small beginnings, the Christian church has grown into a worldwide movement that is still calling persons to follow Jesus, still issuing the invitation to become a disciple of Jesus Christ.*[1]

And so teachers are to be channels of the invitation to accept God's gracious love and live in that love. God, whose very nature is love, then nurtures us as we discover the fullness of being sons and daughters of God.

The miracle of transformation is, from beginning to end, a work of God's grace. The ministry of Christian education and the joyful task of teaching and learning are firmly rooted in that grace. It is God who changes us more and more from our current state of being into the persons God envisions us to be.

When we gather at the baptismal font and when we gather at the Lord's table, we witness to and experience the mystery of God's transforming grace. John Wesley spoke of "walking in the covenant of

How does your educational ministry invite persons to be disciples of Jesus Christ? Who does the inviting? Who is invited?

grace," a vision of the constancy of God's grace which provides both motive and substance for our ministry of Christian education.

Two passages of scripture speak of transformation as an ongoing process of living into God's vision for us. In the first, Paul urges us to open our lives to the work of transformation as he writes:

> *Do not be conformed to this world, but be transformed by the renewing of your minds, so that you may discern what is the will of God — what is good and acceptable and perfect (Romans 12:2).*

To be transformed is to be changed from one way of being to a new way of being. Paul is clear. We can either be conformed to the way of the world, or we can open ourselves to the power of God's transforming grace. If we are willing to do that, our lives can be renewed so that we will be more and more aligned with the will of God, with all that is "good and acceptable and perfect."

The power of the world to mold us is strong. From the moment of birth we are subjected to forces that would conform us to a way of being that is far less than God intends. Paul recognizes the power of those forces in the world around us as they seek to pull us into the vortex of self-will, sin, and abuse. He tells us that God desires more for us and admonishes us to open ourselves to the power of God's transforming grace:

> *I appeal to you therefore, brothers and sisters, by the mercies of God, to present your bodies as a living sacrifice, holy and acceptable to God, which is your spiritual worship (Romans 12:1).*

This verse introduces the theme of transformation in Romans 12:2. We present ourselves to God so that the work of transforming our minds can take place. And we participate in God's work of transforming our

How does your congregation seek to participate in God's transformation of the larger culture?

culture as well as our individual lives. We and our whole world are changed into a new state through the power of God's grace so that we will, more and more, live in faithfulness to God and be able to "discern what is the will of God, what is good and acceptable and perfect."

Through our ministry of Christian education in the congregation we are to create and support, with appropriate resources, a variety of settings for the teaching ministry of the church. The intent of our teaching is to inform and form, to create a space where persons can present themselves to God and where the ongoing work of transformation can take place.

What difference does it make to view our educational ministry as transformational and not just informational?

In the second scripture passage that speaks of transformation, Paul helps us understand that transformation is rooted in God's grace:

> *Now the Lord is the Spirit, and where the Spirit of the Lord is, there is freedom. And all of us, with unveiled faces, seeing the glory of the Lord as though reflected in a mirror, are being transformed into the same image from one degree of glory to another; for this comes from the Lord, the Spirit (2 Corinthians 3:17-18).*

Paul tells us that as we open ourselves to God, as we come to God with "unveiled faces," we participate in a process that is ongoing. He expresses the ongoing nature of that process by saying that we are "being transformed into the same image from one degree of glory to another; for this comes from the Lord the Spirit." As United Methodists we believe with John Wesley that we experience grace at work in our lives in several ways. We move from one experience of grace to another or, as Paul says, from one degree of glory to another.

Our first experience of grace is a subconscious experience that Wesley called *prevenient grace.* That literally means "the grace that comes before."

Prevenient grace is the grace of God that called the world into being. It is the grace that calls us into a relationship with God before we are even aware of God. It is God at work in our lives long before our first glimmer of understanding. It precedes any action or response on our part. Prevenient grace is the grace that prepares us for the dawning awareness that God loves us so much that God seeks us out first.

How have you experienced prevenient grace in your life? In the life of your congregation?

Justifying grace is our next experience of the grace of God in the process of our transformation. Through God's justifying grace made possible in Jesus Christ, we find pardon for sin, liberation from the bondage of guilt, and the possibility of new relationships with God and with one another. Human sin is the condition of our separation from God, and justifying grace takes that sin very seriously. Sin is our being attached and conformed to the way of the world and being separated from God and from God's way for us. We follow the way of the world when we put self before all else, when we use power to achieve our own purpose, and when we participate in corporate willfulness and selfishness. We use the word *sin* to describe all the human behaviors that give evidence of our separation from the God who loves us. Through justifying grace we experience the power of God to turn us around. We are redeemed from the bondage of conformity to the way of the world and set free to pursue the way of God.

How have you experienced justifying grace in your life? In the life of your congregation?

What do you teach about sin in your congregation?

But the turning toward God which comes from God's justifying grace is only the beginning. Sanctifying grace is the lifelong journey toward holiness. This is the experience of God's grace that enables us to grow into the image of Christ and to live as a sign of God's reign among us. Sanctifying grace is purifying grace which restores us day by day, enabling us to love God and neighbor with inward and outward holiness.

How have you experienced sanctifying grace in your life? In the life of your congregation?

John Wesley once likened these experiences of grace to a house. Prevenient grace is the front porch. It invites us to move further in. Justifying grace is the front door. We must move through that door if we are to come into the house and fully experience justifying grace. Sanctifying grace is to live and grow in the house.

We experience God's grace in our lives in countless ways. One of those ways is through the sacraments. God works miracles of grace through the sacraments. Baptism becomes "God's word to us, proclaiming our adoption by grace, and our word to God promising our response of faith and love."[2] The Lord's Supper of bread and wine becomes for us nourishment for the continuing journey of faith.

Teaching is a "means of grace," an outward action which is a channel for conveying God's grace.

How does understanding teaching as a "means of grace" affect your preparation to teach?

God takes the initiative with those who teach and those who learn, preparing the way (prevenient grace) for persons of all ages to hear and to respond to the good news of Christ's saving love (justifying grace) and to grow in holiness (sanctifying grace). God's grace permeates all our teaching and learning. As we teach and as we open ourselves to learn, God's mysterious work of grace happens and all of us — teachers and learners alike — are transformed.

How have you experienced or witnessed a teacher inviting persons to grow in faith in God?

Our ministry of Christian education inspires persons as they hear the wonderful and compelling invitation to open themselves to the possibility of a transformed life. Teachers have the privilege of offering that invitation which can breathe life into persons in their class. Jesus has a passion for us. We see that passion in the Gospel stories which tell of his agony and grief over the death of his friend Lazarus and the way he wept over Jerusalem because the people would not hear God's transforming word. His passion reaches out across the centuries to inspire us and to call us to seek new life.

Our ministry of Christian education also challenges persons as they realize the enormous implications of God's transforming grace. God challenges the present. When we are faithful, we declare to people and to communities that life is not as God intends it to be. We confront that which is alien to the way of God and offer God's grace to persons caught in the trap of those alien ways. There is a better way, a way that incorporates all that is right and good and just and loving. That is God's way for the world. That is the way of God's promise to us, a promise that comes to us most fully through Jesus, the Holy One of God.

Again and again we see Jesus challenge the assumptions of those around him. His challenge invites the listener to begin the journey toward new life. Mark tells about the challenge that came to Simon (who came to be known as Peter) and his brother Andrew.

> As Jesus passed along the Sea of Galilee, he saw Simon and his brother Andrew casting a net into the sea — for they were fishermen. And Jesus said to them, "Follow me and I will make you fish for people." And immediately they left their nets and followed him (Mark 1:16-18).

By accepting Jesus' challenge and invitation, Simon and Andrew enter into a new life. They change their way of living and begin to live more and more in God's way as they join with Jesus to do the work of God in this world. They discover that it is not always an easy life. They struggle to understand this new way of being. They make grievous mistakes. And they persist because they come to know that God's way is, for them, the only way. It is the promised reign of God that they long to know and share with others.

Just as Jesus challenged others with his teaching, so we are called to confront that which alienates persons from God and to declare that God offers a

What assumptions about life and persons exist in your congregation? In your community?

How does Christian education in your congregation challenge the assumptions persons already hold?

better way. God's promises to all people define that better way. By challenging the ways of the world, we can be channels of God's invitation to all people to join themselves to that better way, the coming reign of God.

When we are inspired and challenged, we are led to engagement with God. The task of our ministry of Christian education is to create, support, and provide resources for intentional settings where persons can and will encounter God. These settings should be spaces where God can engage us and where we can engage God, a process that often begins and is enriched as we engage one another.

A living encounter with God transforms lives. David Hunter understood that when he suggested that there are two basic approaches to education.[3] One is a methodology of *detachment* that values only the transmission of information. In this methodology facts from the past are taught in such a way that we can avoid the possibility of God's present activity in our lives. The detachment method assumes that knowledge of the facts is all we need to make informed choices for the future.

On the other hand, the methodology of *engagement* assumes that Christian education happens as we deal with the real issues of our lives. In that process we encounter the God who was not only active in the past, but is still active in the present. Historic encounters with God are important, as they help us understand our present encounters with God. To teach in this way helps us make meaning for our lives out of our own life experience.

The patterns of teaching from our past have often been the patterns of detachment. Only as we learn to teach through engagement will we truly invite persons to know God's transforming grace.

Christian education is a passionate endeavor. God cares passionately about us and about our communities of faith. Leaders and teachers of

Christian education have the privilege of inviting persons to have their lives transformed by God's grace. Their passion for teaching comes from their own experience of God's transforming grace. The invitation to encounter the living God will happen in our communities as people are inspired, challenged, and engaged.

[1]Roy Ryan, *Invitational Teaching* (Nashville: Discipleship Resources, 1988), p. iv.

[2]*The United Methodist Hymnal* (Nashville: The United Methodist Publishing House, 1989), p. 32.

[3]David R. Hunter, *Christian Education as Engagement* (Seabury Press, 1963), Chapter 2.

NOTES

CHAPTER 3
KNOW AND EXPERIENCE GOD AND THE CHRISTIAN FAITH

The scriptures are striking because of the vivid descriptions of ways that people knew and experienced God as present and active in their everyday lives. God was involved in the life of their nation and in all of creation. Those of us who are Christian disciples today are invited to know and experience God as present and active in our everyday lives and in our world.

The invitation is to know God in a uniquely Christian way. The biblical understanding of "knowing" has to do with knowing "who" and knowing "how" as well as knowing "that." In other words, it is an intimate and personal way of knowing God, much like the way we know those we love. It has to do with feelings, emotions, actions, and hopes, as well as information. The Christian way of knowing and experiencing has dimensions of awe and mystery as well as understanding. Just as we are changed by our relationships with the people we love, so we are changed by knowing God. Knowing God involves not only the transmission of information which shapes our understanding, it also involves experience which shapes our very being and all that we do.

The story of God's salvation in creation, through the life of the Hebrew people and in Jesus the Christ, is the story we all need to know. It includes information we need to learn, but it goes beyond that. The

In what ways does your congregation teach the Christian faith as relationship?

stories, language, images, and symbols of our faith also form common memories we all share as Christians. These memories make us a unique people on the journey of faith in this world. Sharing these stories also makes possible effective communication within the community of faith. And perhaps most important, the stories empower us to live as vital congregations and faithful disciples in the world.

The information we learn and teach includes the fact that the Christian faith is not primarily concerned about abstract intellectual issues. The Christian faith is concerned about relationships: with God through Jesus Christ, with one another, and with all of creation. As we allow our lives to be shaped by God and by God's purposes — this Christian way of knowing and experiencing, we grow in our relation-ship with God and discover that we are being shaped more closely in the image of God.

As United Methodists, we believe our knowing and experiencing is grounded in scripture, informed by Christian tradition, enlivened in our experience, and tested by reason.[1]

GROUNDED IN SCRIPTURE

What does your congregation teach about the Bible?

Knowing and experiencing God begins with God's initiative, especially as seen in Jesus the Christ. God's ways and purposes are most clearly revealed in scripture. Through the presence and work of the Holy Spirit, scripture is the primary means by which God's grace can create new relationships with God and with one another, undo our brokenness and bondage, and begin the process of making us whole in Christ. Scripture is the primary source by which our Christian knowing and experience are shaped.

When we, as United Methodists, speak of the primacy or the centrality of scripture, we need to be clear about the nature of scripture and understand what we mean by the authority of scripture.

The original covenant community of God's people and then the renewed covenant community claim that the writings which comprise the Old and New Testaments are "the Word of God." While this claim is open to diverse interpretations, the covenant community of God's people has basically understood this claim to mean that we encounter the living God in scripture. This encounter with God is an experience of entering into the presence of One who is totally and radically outside our values, structures, and dynamics, yet mysteriously present to us in them. God is the One in whose presence all that we know is seen in a completely new perspective.

Scripture is at the same time the Word of God and a human word. God has chosen scripture as one of the primary means for divine self-disclosure; therefore, these words are the Word of God. The United Methodist tradition has always stressed that God is the One who inspired scripture as well as the One we meet in scripture. These words are human words, because God's self-disclosure takes place in the midst of human events that happen in particular historical settings. God's revelation is communicated in human languages by real people who are shaped by their cultural and sociological situation with all its limitation and ambiguity. These human limitations created and continue to create tensions within the communities of believers.

We live in the midst of tremendous diversity — culturally, ethnically, economically, educationally, and politically. God does not speak in a vacuum, but God speaks within the many concrete contexts in which we live. So we approach scripture out of our own particular life-centered settings, each with its own language, traditions, stories, and images. We usually continue to live within these settings as we follow our spiritual pilgrimages. As disciples of Jesus Christ, we take seriously the task of learning how to live in an increasingly multicultural world. This includes

How does the Bible
speak to children in
your congregation?
To youth? To adults?

How does the Bible
speak to persons in
your congregation as
individuals? As a
Christian community?

How does your
church encourage
and support its
teachers to study
scripture?

becoming aware of the variety of ways persons and communities of faith approach the scripture.

However, despite the diversity within which we live, the Bible, through the power of the Holy Spirit, has a defining power for individuals and for communities of faith. For two thousand years distinctive communities have been formed by reading and listening to this Word. Through its new story, new view of reality, and new purpose for being, God seeks to create a new people. The emphasis here is not so much on the words of the Bible, but on the ways God uses those words in the lives of individuals and in the community of faith. The authority of the Bible through the centuries comes from the power of the Holy Spirit through the scriptures to shape and form individuals and communities. When we speak of the inspiration of scripture we mean that the Bible is an indispensable way through which God is made known to us and through which we can experience God's shaping power in our own settings today.

So our educational ministry includes both individual and corporate study of scripture so that all who teach and learn are helped and encouraged to grow toward wholeness in Jesus Christ.

INFORMED BY CHRISTIAN TRADITION

Our knowledge and experience of God are informed by Christian tradition, the accumulation of the church's teaching about God and God's activity in Jesus Christ, in the church, and in all of creation. Our tradition is made up of all kinds of influences and experiences (hymns, stories, language, images) which have informed and formed us in the Christian faith and as United Methodists.

We live within the Christian tradition with its unique language and stories. The Christian tradition is "family history," which is critical to an understanding of who we are. We are surrounded by the saints of the early church, influenced by the creeds hammered out in the great councils of the church, taught by the great theologians such as Augustine and Aquinas, helped to pray by Teresa of Avila and Julian of Norwich, and helped to sing our faith by Bernard of Clairvaux and Beethoven.

John Wesley was convinced that the doctrines that bind Christians together are more important than the things that separate us. He took very seriously the agreements the church had reached through the ages about the Christian faith, and he taught them to his followers. These doctrines are part of the tradition of The United Methodist Church. But our church did not come into being in isolation. We know and experience the Christian faith as shared with other Christians, and Wesley understood that there is much to be learned from them. The unique perspectives and understandings of other Christians can always enrich one another.

The Book of Discipline, 1992 includes both doctrine that we hold in common with other Christians and doctrine that is unique to our Methodist tradition. With others we believe in

- ◆ The trinity, Father, Son and Holy Spirit;

- ◆ The mystery of salvation in and through Jesus Christ;

- ◆ God's redemptive love in the experience of individuals and communities of believers;

- ◆ Our participation in Christ's universal church;

- ◆ The reign of God, both present and future;

- ◆ The authority of scripture;

- ◆ Justification by grace through faith;

- ◆ And the essential oneness of the church of Jesus Christ which is in need of continual reform and renewal.[2]

How can your church help children, youth, and adults catch an excitement about tradition in your congregation and in the Christian community?

As United Methodists, we also have some distinctive doctrines which have emerged out of our tradition. These include

- Prevenient grace;

- Justification and assurance;

- Sanctification and perfection;

- Faith and good works;

- Mission and service;

- Nature and mission of the church.

We can always learn and grow by understanding other traditions, and many of us have come to The United Methodist Church from other traditions. But knowing and experiencing the Christian faith in the Methodist tradition gives us our unique identity among Christians.

What are the traditions and stories of your congregation that are important to pass along to help persons understand who they are as a people of God?

Our educational ministry includes passing on the traditions of the Christian faith from one generation to the next — but there is more at stake than informing people about what the church used to teach. Under the guidance of the Holy Spirit we are also called to explore the meaning of the Christian faith for each new generation. While receiving the agreements that the church has reached over the years, we also explore fresh interpretations of the tradition for ourselves as individuals, for our communities of faith, and for the context within which we live. Our explorations of new understandings always take place in dialogue with the traditions of the church so that we do not too easily fall into error, superficiality, and superstition.

What are some new understandings of the faith emerging for you? For your congregation?

Because of our diversity, we will approach this educational task in a wide variety of ways. But in all of our diversity we will seek to present, clarify, and struggle with God's good news as formative for the time and place within which we live.

ENLIVENED IN EXPERIENCE

Experience has always been a valued part of religious life in our tradition. John Wesley spoke frequently of experience, by which he meant religious experience, especially the converting, confirming experience of new birth in Jesus Christ.

As United Methodists we believe that God's acceptance of us in baptism is the starting point of our faith. When we accept Jesus Christ as Savior and Lord, we begin the journey of bringing all of our experiences under that transforming relationship with God through Jesus Christ. This is the personal appropriation of faith. Our primary experience of God then begins to interpret all of our other experiences, individually and as communities of faith. Our teaching always invites people to explore such questions as: "What claim does this make on your life?" "Where do you find yourself responding?" "Where are you resisting?" This is a call to deal openly and honestly with our religious experience in the faith community.

In addition to being shaped by our relationship with God, our own unique experiences as individuals and communities also shape the ways we know and experience the Christian faith. We are shaped by our geographical location and by our experience of nature, by our political situation of freedom or oppression, by our racial and ethnic origins, and by our gender — and by the ways they influence our roles and status. Our day-to-day experiences are an important lens through which we both know and experience God and our Christian faith. We never exist in a vacuum. God's grace, scripture, and tradition are all mediated through experience.

In our educational task, we take seriously the experiences people bring and the variety of ways in which people will teach and learn. Because of the immense changes taking place in society — political changes, changes in roles and the ways people

TESTIMONIES — leadership

How does your congregation enable an individual's experience of God to become part of the congregation's corporate experience of God?

How does your congregation's corporate experience of God become part of the experience of the individuals who make it up?

relate, changes in our ways of thinking, we cannot approach the teaching and learning task as we have in the past.

To be enlivened by experience is to be invited to discover the wide variety of ways people know and experience God and God's saving grace. It is both challenging and frightening to follow the God who always goes before us and who says to us, "See, I am making all things new" (Revelation 21:5).

TESTED BY REASON

We are called to honor the biblical commandment to love God with all our mind (Matthew 22:37). We approach the teaching/learning task with intellectual vigor and use all of our critical skills. Together we engage in open, inquiring, and disciplined thought, seeking to discover what is idolatrous and what is faithful. Reason undergirds our ability to interpret the Christian faith and our ability to seek its meaning for our time and place. It helps us understand and speak about our experiences of God and the world in which we live. Reason enables us to hear and understand the ancient texts of scripture and tradition and to discover in them new possibilities for our future. A thinking faith will enable us to be faithful to the past, relevant to the present, and viable for the future.

United Methodists have long placed great importance on reasoning as a distinctive human capability. John Wesley wrote and spoke in a clear, rational, and convincing manner. Reason guides us and enables us to keep our ideas consistent. It helps us make connections with the world around us. And perhaps most important, it is reason which enables us to talk about and pass on our knowledge and experience from one generation to another.

How does your congregation respond when children, youth, and adults use God's gifts of reason in ways that challenge assumptions?

Our own experience and scientific research tell us that a "thinking climate" helps individuals and communities grow and mature in their faith. When we use reason, we clarify, elaborate, and connect our faith with our life. It is not a way by which we control the world and other people but a source for understanding the way we live as people of faith in our world. Congregations that nurture a thinking climate engage in teaching and learning that both receive and transform the faith across generations. A thinking faith pays attention to the role of reason, as people and congregations seek meaning for their lives in a changing world.

So the teaching and learning task helps all of us reflect and act on our encounter with God and seek spiritual wisdom for our lives. Our educational ministry invites people and communities of faith to respond to God's good news with lives that are characterized by compassion, courage, justice, mercy, love, and sacrificial service.

To know and experience the God we most clearly meet in Jesus Christ means to be formed into the image of Christ as individuals and as communities of faith. As Christians, we are radically dependent upon the guidance and inspiration of the Holy Spirit. Scripture, tradition, experience, and reason are not ends in themselves. They all serve to enhance our relationship with God, with one another, and with creation, and to continually transform the lives of individuals and communities of faith into that new being which God has envisioned for us all.

How can you improve the "thinking climate" within your congregation?

Big Picture
· Current Events

[1]*United Methodist Book of Discipline, 1992*, p. 40.

[2]Ibid., pp. 42-44.

NOTES

CHAPTER 4
CLAIM AND LIVE GOD'S PROMISES

Rainbows catch our attention. We are often thrilled when we see one and we call others to look at this spectacle in the sky. When we see something as awesome as a double rainbow we cannot keep it to ourselves. Our rainbow stories trigger the telling of favorite rainbow stories by others. The rainbow symbolizes for us the wonder of God's promises to us. God painted a rainbow across the sky as a sign to Noah of the covenant promise made by God to every living creature. Never again would God threaten all of life.

God's grace is the source of God's promises. The grace that seeks us out before we even recognize it, the grace that forgives and offers new life, and the grace that leads us into holiness is the grace on which God's promises rest. We stake our very lives and the meaning of life on God's promises which are the foundation of our relationships with God and with one another. The Psalmist sings:

> *This God — his way is perfect; the promise of the Lord proves true; he is a shield for all who take refuge in him (Psalm 18:30).*

God gives us many promises as expressions of God's love and care for us. Because we trust the one who gives the promises, we trust the promises; and because we trust the promises we can claim them.

As we claim the promises we live them and grow more and more into their fullness.

What do you understand to be the nature of God's promises?

One helpful definition of faith is "trusting in the promises of God." Thomas Droege gives us this definition and speaks of the nature of God's promises:

> *The specific nature of the promise may vary, depending upon particular needs and historical circumstances. To Abraham the promise was descendants as numerous as the stars. To the suffering the promise is God's saving presence and help. To those in exile the promise is a new beginning in a land of promise. To the sick the promise is healing. To the sinner the promise is forgiveness.*
>
> *Despite the variety of forms, the underlying promise is always the same — that God will be present with his life-giving Spirit, his love, and his forgiveness; and will help, restore, bless, and sustain his children.[1]*

What has God promised to your congregation?

GOD WILL BE OUR GOD

This is God's initiating promise, the promise to be our God, a promise made in the very act of creation. God will be our God and we will be God's people. In the decision to create us God makes that promise forever. The wonderful creation stories found in Genesis tell us that God creates man and woman in God's image and breathes life into humankind. God has made us and not we ourselves. This initiating promise, the promise of God to be our God, is made again and again, never more clearly than in the story of Noah:

> *Then God said to Noah and to his sons with him, "As for me, I am establishing my covenant with you and your descendants after you, and with*

*every living creature that is with you, the birds,
the domestic animals, and every animal of the
earth with you, as many as came out of the ark. I
establish my covenant with you, that never again
shall all flesh be cut off by the waters of a flood,
and never again shall there be a flood to destroy
the earth" (Genesis 9:8-11).*

Then God confirms this covenant by offering
the rainbow as a sign that we will be God's people
always and forever.

*God said, "This is the sign of the covenant that
I make between me and you and every living
creature that is with you, for all future generations:
I have set my bow in the clouds, and it shall be a
sign of the covenant between me and the earth"
(Genesis 9:12-13).*

The bow painted across the sky is a reminder to
God, as well as to all humankind, of God's covenant
with all creation.

We claim this initiating promise by continually
remembering who we are. Scripture stories that
tell us of God's loving creation of us and of God's
covenant promises help us remember who we are
and whose we are and begin to tell us how we are
to live.

God Promises to Live in Relationship With Us

This second promise is God's relational promise.
It tells us how God promises to relate to us. The
story of Moses at Mt. Sinai helps us understand
God's promise of relationship. In this story God
gives the ten commandments (Exodus 20-1-21).
These commandments are not just laws to be kept;
they are a promise that God will live in relationship
with us in a special way and expects us to respond
with obedience.

The wonder of this promise is that God chooses to live in relationship to us. And in this story God tells us about the nature of that relationship. God is the Lord, the God who brought the Hebrews out of the land of Egypt, out of the house of slavery. And God sets the boundaries of our relationship with God and with one another.

God first reminds us of the initiating promise, the promise to be our God. Then God reminds us of what God has already done by leading the people out of slavery. God has acted out of great love and care for the people. God then declares that we are to respond to this great love with lives of faithfulness. We are to love and worship God alone. God knows that this relationship will be compromised if someone or something else comes first. God wants our full attention. But that demand goes hand in hand with God's promise of steadfast love to us.

Then we learn how God wants us to relate to one another. That relationship is to be modeled on God's relationship with us. God declares to us that we are not to murder, or to steal, or to covet what another has. We are to be faithful to one another as God is faithful to us.

Jesus comes seeking us out, reminding us again of God's great love and care. Jesus comes to renew God's relationship with us. He comes preaching the good news of God's continuing love for us. He reminds us that God will continually lead us out of whatever bondage holds us captive. In and through Jesus, God reclaims and restates the promise of relationship so that we can come to know and love God and live in that relationship forever. John's Gospel tells us of the boldness of God's seeking love in Jesus Christ:

> For God so loved the world that he gave his only Son, so that everyone who believes in him may not perish but may have eternal life (John 3:16).

In what ways does understanding the ten commandments as based in our relationship with God and with others help your church teach Christian morality to its people?

Jesus' first public teaching reminds his listeners that God seeks out those held in bondage and frees them to live with God when he says:

> The Spirit of the Lord is upon me, because he has anointed me to bring good news to the poor. He has sent me to proclaim release to the captives and recovery of sight to the blind, to let the oppressed go free, to proclaim the year of the Lord's favor (Luke 4:18-19).

Jesus wants his listeners to know that God still seeks us out and longs to live in relationship with us. God still desires us, gives to us the one who will free us from bondage, and invites us to respond to love with love. Jesus reminds us that, if we love God, we also live in loving relationship with all God's people. We claim and live God's relational promise when we live in the same quality of relationship that God puts before us in Jesus, a relationship of love, justice, and faithfulness that frees us from all bondage.

GOD WILL BE WITH US FOREVER

This is God's sustaining promise, the promise of God's continuing presence with us and continuing activity in all creation. Even though we all sometimes experience God as absent rather than present, God has promised to be with us forever. Just as the promises of God are made fresh in Jesus, they are made fresh again and again through the abiding presence of God's Spirit.

In what ways does your congregation understand that God is always present with us?

> If in my name you ask me for anything, I will do it. If you love me, you will keep my commandments. And I will ask the Father, and he will give you another Advocate, to be with you forever (John 14:14-16).

Jesus says these words as he prepares for his death and resurrection. God does not leave us alone.

God is with us in spirit and in truth. God's promise is realized in Pentecost and continues to be realized as God keeps the promise in our lives. God has been, is, and will be forever active in creation. We cannot escape God's eternal presence.

We claim and live the sustaining promise as we make ourselves available to God. Prayer and meditation are ways of being attentive to God, ways we listen for God at work in our lives and in all of creation. We are attentive to God as we seek to be active where God is active. We live in God's sustaining presence when we know that God sees our hearts and when our thoughts and our desires flow from God's love. We look for signs of God's presence and for evidence of the promised reign of God. God's reign is one of justice, love, mercy, and equality. No one is to be excluded. God is the one who empowers us to claim and live the promises in our own lives. When we pray, "Your kingdom come on earth as it is in heaven," we pray with the confidence that God who makes the promise of a new heaven and a new earth is faithful and will keep the promise. God is indeed with us! That is the promise and it is renewed continually by the presence of the Spirit who is with us forever.

> Where do you see evidence of God's reign in your community?

TEACHING THE PROMISES OF GOD

God loves us for who we are, not for what we do. John Wesley, in his exploration of prevenient grace, justifying grace, and sanctifying grace, makes it clear that we do not earn God's grace. That grace is freely given by God. The story of the prodigal son is a powerful story for many of us because the young man does everything wrong in relationship to his father; yet the father loves him and welcomes him home. The meaning of the story is clear to us; yet we often still feel that we must earn God's love. A recent study indicated that two-thirds of the United Methodist respondents had trouble believing that they did not have to earn God's love and grace. We must continue to teach the promise that God's grace is not only freely given but that God's grace has transforming power in our lives. Teachers are called to create the space where persons can hear God's promises and claim them as their own, space where they can wrestle with what it means to live those promises in their daily lives.

Those who teach are to claim and live the promises of God in their own lives, then share the promises through their teaching and their living. Teachers are to claim God's initiating promise and live in the knowledge that we are claimed as God's own. Teachers are called to create the space where class members can come to know God and God's claims on their lives. They do that by telling the stories of God's initiating promise to us and by offering constant reminders that we are claimed by God. Teachers create space as they willingly and boldly claim that they are God's — that God has claimed them, and as they live lives consistent with those claims.

We teach God's relational promise by living out the relationships God offers us and asks of us. This teaching begins by being clear about the nature of the relationships God wants with us and wants us to have with one another and with ourselves. We begin with the youngest persons participating in our ministry of Christian education and continue all through their lives. Helping persons know and remember God's relational promise and the ways that promise can shape our lives is a special task of those who teach.

Teachers also are to claim and live the sustaining promise of God. One of the ways a teacher does that is to expect that God will be at work in the teaching/ learning setting. An adult class was discussing the story about the disciple Thomas and his doubts

Why is it so difficult for persons to believe that they do not have to earn God's love and grace? How might your church's educational ministries overcome those difficulties?

How does your congregation help teachers claim God's promises for themselves?

about Jesus' resurrection. One of the class members
had recently suffered the death of her spouse. She
began to tell the class that in times of suffering it is
often difficult not to doubt God. The teacher was so
intent on getting through the lesson that she could
not allow the person to explore her feelings. The
teacher did not expect the deep emotion of the
woman who spoke, nor did she know what to do with
those feelings. So she simply moved on with the
lesson. God was present in that moment, but the
teacher could not hear and make space for God to
work. Those who teach are to be attentive to the
simple ways that God is present among us.

God promises life, hope and, eternal relationship
with us. God's promises are a constant theme of the
biblical story and are to be a constant theme for
those who teach. God is faithful and keeps all the
promises made to us, but we need constant reminders
of God's faithfulness. Those who teach are called to
be those reminders and thus to encourage others to
know, claim, and live all of the promises of God.

Justo González tells this story of what it means to
claim and live the promises of God:

> Three years ago I was lecturing in Cali, Colombia.
> One afternoon a family took me out to see the
> city — the parents, a son of eighteen, and an
> older daughter who was a seminary student. We
> saw the beautiful avenues and the fancy hotels
> that tourists always see; but we also saw the vast
> sea of cardboard and tin hovels, stretching as far
> as the eye could see. These people have been
> pushed out of their land by drug barons and
> international agribusiness. It had rained that
> week and the whole area was flooded. Human
> excrement floated along the streets in which
> children were playing. The eighteen-year-old boy
> was telling me about a weekly radio program he
> and a group of friends were running. "People in
> Colombia do not know that this exists," he told

me. "So I come to areas like this every week, and I interview people, and on Saturday afternoon I put it on the air. Some people don't like it."

Some time later, when the father and I were alone, he looked at me with tear-filled eyes and said, "They'll probably kill him for what he is doing." I thought his next words would be, "It's terrible how these young people get such ideas in their heads." But no, he smiled and said: "But we are Christians. I raised him for this. I must share his dream."

This is what it means to claim and live the promises of God — the initiating promise, the relational promise, and the sustaining promise. God promises that people held in bondage will be set free, and we are called to be a part of making that promise a reality. This family in Colombia is doing more than dreaming. They are living as if the reign of God is at hand, and for them it is. Death may come, but they know that death cannot and will not separate them from the promise of God, the promise of eternal relationship to the One who is Love.

Living the promises of God is not always so dramatic. This story shows that God's call to us is to claim the promises and to live faithfully in our ordinary lives.

What opportunities does your church provide to help children, youth, and adults live the promises of God?

A pastor told about a woman in a congregation he served early in his ministry. Shortly after arriving, he went to visit this woman who kept all of the membership and attendance records for the church and faithfully called to check on those who were absent. As they talked, she said to him, "I can't teach Sunday school and I can't be the president of United Methodist Women and I can't hold an office in the church, but I can keep these records." She told him that she had a daughter who was mentally disabled and needed constant care. Her daughter was now middle-aged and continued to need her mother's care. The woman talked about her love for God and for the church. For her, keeping the records, which she could do at home, was her proper response to God's good gifts. She knew the promises of God, and she taught that young pastor what it meant to know, claim, and live those promises day by day.

Claiming and living the promises of God can be dramatic and lead us to places and actions we never dreamed were possible for us. Claiming and living the promises of God can also mean accepting the ordinary lives that we live day by day. God claims us as God's own and promises to be with us. We respond by claiming what we know of those promises and by living them out as fully as we can at every moment of our lives.

In ordinary and extraordinary ways we tell of God's promises. As teachers and leaders, as parents and disciples, we proclaim God's promises and encourage others to claim and live them now. Paul reminds us that we who call Christ Savior and Lord can trust the promises of God.

For in him every one of God's promises is a "Yes." For this reason it is through him that we say the "Amen," to the glory of God (2 Corinthians 1:20).

[1]Thomas A. Droege, *Faith Passages and Patterns* (Minneapolis: Augsburg Fortress Press, 1983), p. 25. Reproduced by permission of Augsburg Fortress.

NOTES

CHAPTER 5
GROW AND SERVE AS CHRISTIAN DISCIPLES

The United Methodist Church has always had a deep commitment to helping individuals and communities pattern their lives after the life of Christ. This includes a call to make visible our love of God and neighbor. This chapter explores some of the ways our growth into Christ is nurtured by our service to God and to our neighbor.

GROW AS CHRISTIAN DISCIPLES

We grow in our faith as we experience God's grace transforming our daily lives. Vitality and fullness of life replace emptiness and meaninglessness. As our knowledge of God and of the Christian faith increases, and as our commitment to Christ grows deeper, we are able to continue living faithful lives.

Growth follows birth and is a natural part of the life cycle. That is true in our spiritual as well as in our physical lives.

> *Like newborn infants, long for the pure, spiritual milk, so that by it you may grow into salvation (1 Peter 2:2).*

Watching an infant grow is one of the most exciting experiences in life. We do not expect infants to think, act, and react in the same way that adults do. But we do expect infants to grow and progress, and it is heartbreaking when an infant does not develop normally.

In our physical lives we expect growth and change in order to express and enjoy life. Our spiritual lives are no different. Growing spiritually is an exciting adventure. As individuals and as communities, we change, we are renewed, and we share in renewing God's creation every day. As Christians who claim life in the power of the Holy Spirit, we live and rejoice in what God already has done, what God is doing, and what God wants for us. Spiritual growth is a lifelong process, and spiritual disciplines are the means by which we continue that process.

We Grow Into Christ

Our journey of faith begins wherever we are. We bring with us the questions, concerns, doubts, and affirmations that we hold about God and about our own lives. God does not let go of us until God has made us over into new persons. God's renewing work takes place in us each day, and each day we find out new things about our humanity. Some of what we learn is pleasant and some is not. This journey is filled with new challenges and new tasks along the way.

God's vision for our spiritual growth is that we become like Christ. Our knowledge of God, our personal and communal characters, our actions, and our reactions are to be shaped in the image of Christ. That is what it means to become mature Christians, filled with the fruit of righteousness, with love and joy and peace. God's loving work in our lives does not happen overnight. Maxie Dunnam said, "We may be converted to Christ in the miracle of a moment, but becoming a saint is the task of a lifetime."[1] Spiritual growth is the lifelong process of having our lives conformed to the life of Christ.

The early Methodists talked about "sanctification" or "going on to perfection." They meant that by grace we grow into Christ and live lives that are patterned after the perfection of Christ. Loving God and one's neighbors is the highest obligation of that life. Christian perfection also means that God's grace and love can make our lives complete, good, and useful. That is life as God intends it to be.

No one is ever too old, too pure, too holy, or too righteous to continue growing into Christ. A woman became a widow at the age of forty. She had a sixteen-year-old child to support and, since she had not previously worked outside the home, she was uncertain where to turn. She tried working as a clerk in a jewelry store, but she was not cut out to be a salesperson. She had taught Sunday school since she was fourteen and had always wanted to become a teacher. But she had married, and resources were scarce during the Depression, so she had not achieved her goal. At the urging of friends and family, she entered college at the age of forty-one. Her daughter was a classmate and her study coach. In two years she earned her associate degree and was able to teach full time and continue her college courses in the evenings and summers. Finally, in 1962, she graduated from college. Her teaching career lasted eighteen years, and she influenced the lives of hundreds of first graders.

We Grow in the Context of Community

Christian education is the congregation's systematic and intentional effort to create, to support, and to provide resources for settings in which the ministry of teaching takes place. As Christians, we identify ourselves with the community of believers and its mission and purpose, and we bind ourselves to one another through a covenant of love. God's redemptive love unites us with Christ in the church.

What does your church teach about Christian perfection? What opportunities are made available to help individuals and the community of faith grow?

How does your congregation support lifelong learning?

We are a gathering of strangers who have come together because we have heard God call our name and we want to follow Christ. God does not call us as isolated individuals to a way of believing; God calls us into community, to a way of life together.

Our faith grows best in a community of believers, which supports us and holds us accountable. The Christian tradition has always valued and protected the worth of each individual person, but it has also asserted that we as individuals are most fully alive in the context of the Christian community. So the ministry of Christian education in the congregation plays a key role in our growth and in equipping us to serve.

What are the marks of your Christian community?

In Acts 2:42, 44-47, Luke describes the life of the early Christian community. The marks of that community are as important for the church today as they were at the time of the first Christian Pentecost.

The church Luke describes was a lively, active church. The faith of those first Christians was not just a cognitive faith or a set of beliefs but a living faith that immersed them in the world in which they lived.

The church of Pentecost lived day by day. Becoming and being the church was a twenty-four-hour, seven-day-a-week matter for those first Christians. The ministry that eventually became known as Christian education was the church's way of equipping persons for this total immersion in the faith of Jesus Christ, while living within a world often hostile to that faith. They heard the apostles' teachings in ways that touched their feelings, actions, values, relationships, and desires, as well as their understandings. We, too, are to present the whole story of God in Christ to the whole person.

The church of Pentecost lived rhythmically. Believers came together for worship and mutual support, then moved apart to witness and to serve. Although the early church appointed particular persons to different tasks (Acts 6:2), all members of

the church were involved in the life-giving cycle of
serving the world and being served by the community of the faithful. This rhythm was a natural result
of the apostles' teachings which included both
nurture and outreach.

Luke's description suggests that it was the
church's attentiveness to the apostles' teaching, to
prayer, and to fellowship, all guided by the Holy
Spirit, that empowered the people to be the church
in the world at that time. The ways those first-
century Christians attended to the apostles' teaching
and to fellowship came to be known as the ministry
of Christian education.

◆ They grew as disciples by devoting
   themselves to the apostles' teachings,
   especially those about the life, teachings,
   death, and resurrection of Jesus Christ.

◆ They grew as disciples in a community of
   persons called into covenant and bound first
   and primarily by their belief in Jesus Christ.

◆ They grew as disciples by spending time
   together in the church, by breaking bread at
   home and eating together, by praising God
   and having the goodwill of the people.

◆ They grew as disciples by giving their earthly
   goods to provide physical comfort for those
   who were suffering and by reaching out to the
   world with the Good News, the story of Jesus
   Christ.

◆ They grew as disciples through the life-
   giving and life-sustaining rhythm of active
   involvement in the world balanced by regular
   withdrawal into the community of believers
   for support.

All of these dimensions of their common life —
sharing the teachings of the apostles, building

Christian fellowship, hearing and responding to God's call to serve, providing encouragement for one another through prayer — became formalized over time into dimensions of the ministry of Christian education.

We Grow in Faith

How does your church help people see that they must grow in faith?

As Christians we have heard God's call and have answered that call by making appropriate vows of commitment. We are faithful to those vows, and we grow in faith when we intentionally cultivate and nurture our spiritual development. We are not satisfied with staying the way we are. Growth in faith involves looking at the things about ourselves that we want to change. At the beginning of our spiritual journeys, we are not very much like Christ. We need to help each other, just as an infant needs help when he or she is born into a family.

In what ways does your congregation hold people accountable and support them as they grow in faith?

In order to help each other grow, Korean Methodist congregations (including Korean United Methodist congregations) have retained the tradition of class meetings which provide a framework for accountability and mutual support in Christian discipleship. Every member of a class meeting learns the meaning of being a Christian and is held account- able weekly for doing works of devotion, worship, compassion, and justice. New members are encour- aged and guided by old members to choose a life that puts Jesus Christ at the center.

God is the source of our growth, and God's Spirit works within us through Bible study, worship, and the activities of our common life. Through our study we learn the ways that God works in the world and relates to us. Both personal and corporate worship nurture our relationship with God. As we live out God's call to work for justice through our active involvement in the church, God changes and reshapes us.

All of these dimensions shape our way of living. The Christian life has a distinctive rhythm and pattern, including such activities as regular devotional reading, weekly attendance at worship and Christian education classes; regular participation in Holy Communion; special seasonal celebrations; visitation of homebound members; volunteer work with programs for those in need; and promotion of racial, cultural, and gender inclusiveness.

When we join The United Methodist Church, we promise to support it with our prayers, our presence, our gifts, and our service. This is our response to God's call in our lives. We invest ourselves in the mission of Christ in the world by developing intimacy with God, with others, and with ourselves. We reject old forms of existence and accept new forms. We live out our promise by expressing our commitment to Christ in our daily lives. Because we live every day knowing we have been freed by the forgiving love of God, we are empowered to share that love with others and to work for justice in the world.

All of us grow in our own faith when we offer it to others and when others nurture our faith. Christian education is the lifelong journey of teaching and being taught, of growing and encouraging others to grow.

SERVE AS CHRISTIAN DISCIPLES

Jesus commanded disciples to "love the Lord your God with all your heart, and with all your soul, and with all your mind" and "your neighbor as yourself" (Matthew 22:37, 39). Our service to God and to God's creation is rooted in these two great commandments. It is essential, not optional. It results from our commitment to Christ; it is rooted in our identity as his followers; and it is empowered by God's transforming grace. God's commandment does not require legalistic obedience, but it calls forth our gratitude for God's grace which is expressed in our

How does your church's educational ministry encourage and support persons to act in Christian service?

attitudes and actions. This is the "obedience of faith" to which Paul referred in Romans 1:5:

> *Through whom we have received grace and apostleship to bring about the obedience of faith among all the Gentiles for the sake of his name.*

What does your church teach about the relation between good works and faith?

United Methodists have always linked faith and works. John Wesley believed that doing good works, giving ourselves to others, and using our wealth to help others were ways of expressing our Christian faith and nurturing its growth.

Christianity is not a list of rules to be followed or dogmas to be believed. God calls us together to share our goods, to sustain one another, and to support our common life. Not only the gifts we receive from others but also the gifts we give to them will nurture and sustain our growth in faith. We share our faith in order to keep it, and we need each other to continue in the path of discipleship.

We are co-workers with God who invites us to claim the world as God's own, the place where God is at work. We join in God's transforming work and we witness to God's grace in our own lives knowing that we are dependent upon God's power and guidance. It is God's work we do, not our own.

We Render Service

In our ministry of Christian education we are to make visible the many and varied forms of service to which God calls us. We are ordinary Christians who can help others know and understand the Christian life through our words and our actions. But two temptations constantly confront us. The first is that we will focus too much on our own satisfaction and status as givers. The second is that we will leave the task to someone else. These temptations may keep us from accepting the charge Christ has given and cause us to betray the essential nature of Christian service.

Our service takes a variety of forms:

PRAYER: There is no more basic form of service than prayer. In this place we encounter God and God's grace comes to us. Prayer arises from our deepest desire to know and love God and to be known and loved by God. It quiets us and opens us to the reality of God in our lives.

Even though prayer is personal, it can never be privatistic. Through prayer we reach out to others and embrace the world. Prayer changes us and those for whom we pray so that we can hear the call to discipleship and carry out the command to love others. We know that we serve only through the power of love in Jesus Christ. Prayer is our response of gratitude for the undeserved gift of love. In our individual and communal prayer we acknowledge and surrender to God's power, center our lives on God's unconditional love, and become a channel of God's love to others. We pray for discernment in understanding our responsibility for the world and for obedience in carrying out that responsibility.

WITNESS: When we witness to God's great love, we move out from the community of believers to confront injustice and to offer God's grace to people who are estranged from God. We proclaim and offer to others the transforming love of Jesus Christ that we know in our own lives. Our witness takes place in the face of constant pressure from the world to conform to its ways. Our witness for Christ takes courage and discipline, and we know that it is not an option but a responsibility.

Early Methodists were often harassed and ridiculed, not because of their theological positions, but because of their brave witness against unjust social structures. John Wesley's great concern for social holiness led them to courageous communal witness for Christ in the midst of human misery. They spoke out against slavery. They fought against child labor and for collective labor bargaining during the early twentieth century. And the Social Principles have been a powerful statement of the church's concern for justice since the early years of this century.

RECONCILIATION: Our commitment to service in the name of Jesus Christ flows from the reconciliation we know in our own lives. As Christians we proclaim reconciliation to a divided world as we experience our own redemption through Jesus Christ. We are able to offer reconciliation to others as we experience reconciliation within our own community of believers. The transforming grace of God that we know in our own lives — the grace which seeks us out, forgives us daily, and shapes our lives in the image of Christ — that prevenient, justifying, and sanctifying grace is also at work transforming the life of our congregation. It is not always easy to allow that grace to work in our midst. To be reconciled with one another when there are tensions and disagreements among us is often difficult and painful. But it is one of the most important ways that we make visible God's transforming love. Without the empowering grace of God, our witness can be destroyed by bitterness and strife in our midst. But with that grace, our community of faith can become a sign of God's reign in the midst of a hurting world.

CARE OF THE LEAST: One of the most profound teachings of the Bible is that we cannot worship God in isolation from our relationships with one another, especially the least of God's creatures. Their welfare is God's special concern, and we are God's partners in ministry with and for them. The unconditional love God has given us calls us to give ourselves unconditionally to those who are in need. In doing so, we discover that God empowers us to serve by giving us strength and patience, and even delight, in caring for God's own. We also discover that the gifts we receive far exceed anything we can give. In offering hospitality to those who are fearful strangers, we often find that the guest becomes the host and we are the recipients of great gifts. When we give of our financial and material resources, know that whatever we have has been received from God in trust and thus can be given freely.

Perhaps most important, service in the name of Jesus Christ always treats the least and the lost as loved and valued persons, not as objects of charity. After all, we are serving Christ himself (Matthew 25:35-36).

TEACHING: Teaching is a unique way of serving through which we offer to others the foundations of the Christian faith and the richness of our own personal story. Our teaching ministry helps persons discern and discover what God is calling them to do and to be. It gives precious opportunities for listening to God and responding in service to others. Our teaching ministry equips persons to live as Christians and to be ready for the constant transitions of life's journey. We all face conflicts in our personal and corporate lives, often with more doubt and confusion than clarity and certitude. In such times we confront our weakness and vulnerability. We are tempted to deny our pain rather than remain open to where it might lead us. Our teaching ministry can be a wonderful source of strength to people struggling to remain faithful in such times. Not only those in crisis, but also those who teach, grow in their own faith as they offer it to others.

We Count the Cost

Being a disciple of Jesus Christ is not easy. Discipleship is costly and often requires that we give up things the world has taught us to value. Jesus taught his disciples that they were to take up a cross and carry it in self-sacrifice. But when we have experienced the transforming power of God's grace

How might your
church's teaching
ministry affirm both
God's unconditional
love and costly
discipleship?

in our own life, we know that our commitment to
Jesus Christ is of far greater value than the things we
give up. Thus, our discipleship and service are not a
burden but a privilege.

We are called to become personally and
corporately involved in the lives of others, knowing
that our involvement will require sacrifice. We cannot
proclaim God's action in Christ and sit by while some
perish in physical or spiritual poverty. We cannot
have God in our hearts without letting God use our
hands to do God's work in the world. All members of
the body of Christ are constrained through love to
bear witness to God and to pray for others. God
commands a service of love and gives the love to
empower that service. This inner relation between
commandment and love is what makes the service
of Christians distinctive.

WE LIVE IN THE PROMISE OF GOD

Human existence has three time dimensions —
past, present, and future. As Christians, our lives are
shaped by these three dimensions of time. We live
out of the past because our faith is grounded in what
God has done in the past through generations of
faithful people, especially those in the Bible. We live
in the present because our faith is grounded in what
God is doing in our lives through the love revealed to
us in Jesus Christ. We live toward the future because
our faith is grounded in hope. We live in the promise
of God, confident that divine promise will be fulfilled.

As Christians, we believe that our faithful love and
service to God and God's creation involve us in the
fulfillment of God's purposes for creation. We are able
to live and to serve confidently in the present because
of God's promise in Jesus Christ — the promise that
we will find wholeness of life through the grace of God.

[1]Maxie D. Dunnam, *The Workbook on Spiritual Discipline*
  (Nashville: The Upper Room, 1993), p. 8.

✠ NOTES

CHAPTER 6
SHAPE OUR MINISTRY OF CHRISTIAN EDUCATION

From the first splash of color on the canvas comes a beautiful painting, and from the first patches of cloth stitched together comes an intricate and unique quilt. In the same way, each community of faith shapes its ministry of Christian education, and the creation which flows from the foundation becomes more beautiful and more intricate. In this chapter we will explore some ways in which these foundations can become a source for enabling and empowering Christian education in local congregations. To do this we will focus on three fundamental concerns of Christian education:

1. Teachers in our ministry of Christian education

2. Settings for our ministry of Christian education

3. Curriculum and our ministry of Christian education

TEACHERS IN OUR MINISTRY OF CHRISTIAN EDUCATION

Teaching is the heart of Christian education. How do we in our local congregations insure that our heart will be strong? We start by answering the question, "Why do we teach?"

Why do *you* teach?

61

We teach because God calls us to teach. We teach because we believe that people can be transformed. We teach because we have a passionate desire to invite persons to grow in faith through Jesus Christ. We teach because people need a faith which influences their every thought and every action. We teach to help people find meaning and purpose in life and to reflect theologically on their day-to-day experiences. We teach because we know faithful teaching builds congregations that are vital and faithful. We teach because people and congregations need a clear sense of identity as a people of God and as United Methodists.[1]

All persons in the Christian community of faith are both teachers and learners. Pascal once said, "One Christian is no Christian." Christian education happens in community. As Christians we have both an individual and corporate identity. When we say, "I am a child of God," we also say, "I belong to a people of faith." The Bible gives witness to this community and helps us understand what it means to be God's people. As United Methodists we believe that we are all called to teach and to witness. Every time we gather to celebrate a baptism, we renew our common commitment to that calling. Through our congregational vows we say, "You cannot do this alone. We are here for you, to guide you, to teach you, to learn with you as a community seeking to live lives faithful to the gospel of Jesus Christ." All of us teach and learn simply by living with one another.

However, part of the function of the community is to help persons understand their own special gifts and talents. The congregation lifts us up, names our gifts, helps us to discern our calling, and supports us in exercising these gifts for the church and on behalf of the whole world. Thus all of us, as both teachers and learners, have responsibility for the teaching ministry of our congregation. One important aspect of that responsibility is to identify and then to invite those who may be called to be teachers.

Inviting Teachers

If we are to help call forth persons to teach, then we must be sure that our definition of teacher is not too narrow. Sometimes we think that only those who teach in formal settings such as Sunday morning classes or weekday Bible studies are teachers. But, in reality, teachers of the faith are many and varied. Some may not even realize that they are teachers. Teachers include persons who teach on Sunday mornings, but they also include those who teach in the home and in one-to-one conversations, pastors who teach through their sermons, worship leaders who teach in corporate worship, youth group advisors, camp counselors, and many others.

We give power to the name *teacher* when we show that we value that name. When we help people in these various settings see themselves as teachers of the faith, we increase the effectiveness of our ministry of Christian education.

Identifying teachers not only means naming those who are functioning as teachers; it also means calling forth persons to teach in particular settings. In order to do that, we must have a broad vision of who might be effective teachers. We know that effective teachers are people of faith, but we do not assume that those who know the most about the Bible and religion have the strongest faith. Nor should we assume that those who know the most about teaching techniques will be the best teachers. Of course it is important to teach the content of the Bible, church history, doctrine, and the language and practice of our faith. However, this will not neces-sarily guarantee that those we teach will grow in faith. Teaching which does not look at the world in

How does your church identify and secure teachers?

I, Timothy

which we live and help persons make decisions for living faithfully in the struggles of their daily lives will not effectively nurture their faith. We are called to teach and live in such a way that the world and its many problems are embraced in faith instead of ignored. Teachers who are also learners, and who are struggling to live faithfully in their own lives, will support and nurture faithful living in others.

A recent research project identified these traits of effective teachers:

What other traits of effective teachers can you identify?

- *A willingness to grow and learn along with those whom they teach.*

- *A knowledge of their students — their likes and dislikes, their joys and sorrows.*

- *A knowledge of how people learn and grow through life stages.*

- *A faith that is seen not only in the words they speak, but in their actions in the congregation and the larger community.*

- *A growing knowledge of the Bible and a willingness to continue studying and pondering the scriptures.*

What opportunities are there in your congregation for teachers to share their own faith journeys with one another? To share their joys and challenges in teaching?

- *A teaching style which invites others into the learning situation and awakes in them a desire to know God as they see God known by their teacher.*[2]

Knowledge of content and teaching methods is helpful, but as you can see by this list, it is by no means the only or perhaps even the most important factor in selecting teachers. Only if we have a broad understanding of effective teaching can we help persons in our congregation hear and respond to God's call to teach.

Many teachers might say, "Oh, yes. I had a call to teach. It came late one night and the voice on the other end said, `We're desperate. Could you please teach?'" God's call just might come in that way. But it also happens as a congregation prayerfully considers the need for teachers, and names and faces occur to them in their time of prayer. And it happens through casual conversations where we begin to think and consider what teachers have done for us in the past and what we might do for others. It happens as pastors and diaconal ministers challenge persons to consider how great the need for teachers is in their congregation. And of course it happens through Bible study and worship where the call to service is explored. Congregations as communities of faith help us and others hear and respond to God's call to teach.

When there was no youth teacher, the youth at one church were called together. They talked about what they wanted their class to be and what they hoped would happen when they came together. They named the qualities they wanted in the person who would work with them. Then they answered the question, "Who in our congregation have we described?" They immediately came up with a name and went to invite that person to teach their class. He accepted.

Supporting Teachers

Effective teaching occurs when we have a system of support for teachers that values them and their teaching and equips them to be even more effective. When a congregation understands that the purpose of Christian education is to transform people and communities, then teachers, learners, and all of us know why teaching is so important. When the value of teaching is proclaimed in the congregation, then teachers know they are important. And when the whole congregation celebrates the ministry of teaching, they help create a climate where learning can take place.

How do church members know what is happening within the church's educational ministries?

How does the congregation dedicate and recognize teachers?

One Sunday morning a man visited a congregation for the first time. He came in early for worship and, as many of us do, watched people as they entered. Several people carried totebags. He was curious about them and, when someone with one of the bags sat nearby, he read the message on the side: "Proud to Be a Sunday School Teacher." In a very concrete way, this congregation was saying to the teachers, "Stand up and be noticed. You're one of our teachers and we value you." All who saw the totebags knew that this congregation believes teaching is important.

Pastors can also play a special role in supporting the ministry of Christian education. They do so first when they have a vital faith and are deeply committed to Christ and to their calling in ministry. When they are themselves involved in lifelong learning, they communicate the importance of that to their congregation. These are pastors who devote hours to the Christian education program. This might be through their own teaching, through leadership with those who teach, through sermons that say again and again to the congregation, "We are a learning, growing congregation where all are expected not only to be a part of corporate worship but to be a part of a Christian education class."

What role does your pastor (or pastors) play in the educational ministry of your congregation?

Pastors who know how persons learn will work to see that classes, buildings, and teaching techniques reflect this knowledge. They will have a vision for what the congregation can do and be through the participation of persons of all ages in Christian education. Pastors can help build this vision by bringing concerns for teaching and learning to committees, work groups, and study groups and by helping them address these concerns throughout the work of the congregation. Many congregations also have diaconal ministers and other educators on their staff. Those persons are also important leaders in bringing to reality a vision for Christian education.

Each congregation shows that it values the ministry of teaching by carefully planning ways to express support for teachers. We can do this by offering training so teachers can understand and appropriate their faith heritage and learn skills to help them communicate their faith in appealing ways to those they teach. We can support them with services of recognition, opportunities to speak in worship, times to share with others who teach, and opportunities to renew and reaffirm their commitment to teaching with the support of the whole congregation.

We also support teachers when we equip them to do their work. They need to know that their own growth is essential and not optional. "If teaching is to be taken seriously, a congregation must begin to be increasingly clear about the experience, preparation, and commitment it requires of its teachers."[3] We can do this in a variety of ways:

What do you expect of teachers in your church? How are those expectations communicated?

- By providing prayer partners for teachers

- By purchasing books which help teachers in their own spiritual growth

- By providing substitutes once a quarter so teachers can sit down together in a class led by the pastor

- By sending teachers to district and conference training events, laboratory schools, and national events

- By supporting teachers and students in their involvement with community issues

In what other ways might your congregation support teachers?

Our support says clearly to all who teach, "What you are doing is life-changing and vital for us." One critical way we do this is by reminding people that learning happens at every age and stage of life. Adults are as much in need of Christian education as are children and youth. Maria Harris says,

The first misunderstanding is that education is for children. This misunderstanding is so deep that when we try to speak of education that is not for children, we must give it a name such as "adult" education to distinguish it from the (so-called) real thing. But the truth of education is that if it is assumed to be only for children, it will not be good for anyone — especially not for children.[4]

If we truly believe this, we will equip teachers to teach in ways that are appropriate to each age level and to different ways of learning. Because we take seriously the life-changing nature of Christian education, we will create a community that nurtures faith by emphasizing life experiences as occasions for spiritual insight. We will recognize the unique faith journey of each individual, knowing that faith is whole and complete for persons of all ages. We will be concerned for the world and will seek to learn what God asks of us in the concrete situations we face. We will strongly encourage independent thinking and questioning. We will create opportunities for what one educator, Jack Seymour, calls "theology at sunset," his image for biblical and theological study that connects the text with the daily work that has just ended. All of that means providing educational choices and using a variety of ways of teaching.

How do you help teachers identify and enrich their teaching style?

One of the most important ingredients in our support for teachers is the opportunity for them to engage in interpreting the tradition in terms of their own life experience. Teaching is an act of interpretation by the teacher as well as encouraging interpretation by the learners. If we are serious about nurturing teachers who can help others link faith and life, we can do so by helping those teachers reflect and interpret their own lives in relationship to God's grace.

Effective teachers care deeply for the persons in their class or their group and for others as well. They know that people come seeking more than knowledge. They want a place to belong, people who care, and opportunities to care for others. All of us, children, youth, and adults, need to know that we matter. We support our teachers by caring for them and making them aware of the importance of their caring for the persons they teach. Only if they intentionally provide that kind of care will others grow and respond to God's love.

All of these ways of valuing and equipping teachers occur in the local congregation. As a connectional church, United Methodists believe that support is important not only through the local congregation, but also through the annual conference and general church agencies. Annual conferences can provide critical support to ministries of Christian education. They do this by taking seriously their role in preparing ordained clergy and lay professionals for service in local congregations. Annual conferences can provide conference-wide experiences for training, support, and motivation of teachers. And they can promote effective Christian education as a goal for every local congregation.

Support for teachers and teaching continues at the general church level. The General Board of Discipleship provides resources to help local congregations assess their ministry of Christian education and train their leaders. The Curriculum Resources Committee and Church School Publications develop curriculum materials for use in our local congregations.

SETTINGS FOR OUR MINISTRY OF CHRISTIAN EDUCATION

Our faith is nurtured in a variety of places — a Sunday morning class, a camp in the mountains, a *Disciple* group, congregational worship, a weekday preschool class, or a conference youth rally.

What information does your church gather about its students? How does it use that information to enhance learning?

Describe some ways in which your annual conference supports teachers in your church.

Likewise, a family gathering at home where we read and discuss the Bible together or a work team of church members at the local recycling center are both places of learning and nurture. Just as we believe that people learn in a variety of ways, we believe that people meet God in a variety of places. An effective ministry of Christian education will offer many places where teaching and learning occur.

In our planning we look first at the whole congregation as the larger setting in which our ministry of Christian education takes place. In order to be effective, our congregation will have a climate for learning that encourages telling the Christian story and appropriating that story in our own lives so that we grow as disciples of Jesus Christ. Only then can we move on to look at particular settings.

As we plan, we will be certain that we do not limit Christian education to formal Sunday morning classes separated into age groups. The teaching and learning that can happen in these settings is important; however, not every learner will find this setting appealing, and not every person in our congregation can attend at this time. In our culture, work is not limited to 9:00-to-5:00 or Monday-through-Friday, and many who would be church members cannot attend on Sunday mornings. We must provide a wide array of places and styles of teaching in order to meet the needs of as many people as possible.

In recent years we have often neglected the home as a setting for Christian education. We have said that parents are the primary educators of their children, but we have set up church programs to take every available minute of family time. We have not offered support by providing materials for home study use. Nor have we recognized the home as the center for Christian education for age groups other than children. Reclaiming the home as a primary setting is important in carrying out our ministry of Christian education.

How does your congregation continue to plan for and provide appropriate settings for each potential learner?

CURRICULUM AND OUR MINISTRY OF CHRISTIAN EDUCATION

Defining Curriculum

The word *curriculum* comes from the Latin verb *currere*, which means "to run." Taken literally, then, curriculum means a course to be run. Over the years we have used the word in many different ways. We sometimes talk about curriculum as our total experience of Christian nurture. In this sense, every setting, every person, every printed item, and every piece of equipment not limited to the classroom situation is curriculum. The curriculum becomes a person's total experience within the community of believers, the church. Worship and the sacraments, the sermon and a pastoral call, classroom experiences and fellowship meals — all are part of the curriculum. While there is truth in this view, it is too broad for our purposes in this document. Perhaps a better way to understand the total life of the congregation is as the learning environment in which we are nurtured.

We also sometimes understand curriculum in too narrow a sense, seeing it only as a set of materials — the books for teachers and students. It is more accurate to speak of these as curriculum *materials,* recognizing that they are only a part of the whole curriculum for education in the church.

For our purposes, curriculum is *the design or plan for education in our congregation.* We base this plan on the definition, purpose, and affirmation of Christian education on pages 3-7 in the first chapter. Curriculum materials are developed to help carry out the general plan or design for Christian education in our particular congregation.

Because we are learning all the time, we are not always aware of everything that is going into our design for learning. We need to examine as carefully as possible what we are actually presenting that is part of our plan. We also become aware of what we are unintentionally presenting or have left out of our plan. We refer to these as the *explicit* curriculum and the *implicit* curriculum.

What are you *explicitly* teaching?

Our explicit curriculum is that which is actually presented, consciously and with intention. For example, when we teach the story of the good Samaritan, the facts we present, the pictures we use, the songs we sing, and the activities we plan are all part of our explicit curriculum.

What are you *implicitly* teaching?

The implicit curriculum occurs through the room design, attitudes, and learning styles we use. We may not think of this as teaching, but all of us learn with each of these things. Some implicit curriculum teaches by its presence and some by its absence. For example, a room design with the teacher standing in front of a group of students implicitly teaches, "I have the answer. I will tell you what you are to learn and you will learn it." Or in the telling of the good Samaritan, the questions we choose to ask teach implicitly. When we ask questions that require reciting back the facts of the story, we teach the learners that it is important to know the story as it happened. These are examples of implicit curriculum that teaches by its presence. If we ignore questions about what the story of the good Samaritan means for life today, we teach that Bible stories are only for the past and do not help us live today. And if we fail to provide pictures of faithful people from a variety of cultures, a variety of places in the world, and a variety of ages, we teach that our faith is for people who look like us, act like us, and live like us. These are examples of implicit curriculum that teaches by its absence.

What are you *not* teaching?

Implicit curriculum is not limited to content. If men are not serving as teachers in a particular congregation, then both boys and girls begin to get the message that education is only for women. And if we do not provide a variety of activities in a teaching design, we teach our students that their opinions, preferences, and learning styles are not important.

It is important to examine and re-examine what we teach explicitly, what we teach implicitly, and what we are leaving out. All of these form our attitudes, values, and beliefs, and determine what we learn and do not learn about being faithful disciples.

Developing Curriculum

The development of United Methodist curriculum for Christian education involves many people. The first stage takes place at the general church level, and it takes place in two steps: (a) The Curriculum Resources Committee of the General Board of Discipleship develops the church's general curriculum plan. This overall plan establishes objectives for systematic study settings for persons at all ages, and for a wide range of family, parent, intergenerational, and age-level informal learning groups. (b) A wide range of specific curriculum materials is then developed and made available to congregations. These materials help carry out the purpose and affirmations of Christian education in congregations.

A second stage in curriculum development takes place in local churches. As part of the design for Christian education, the work area on education or nurture determines the best kinds of curriculum materials for the ministry of Christian education in that congregation. We then secure the most appropriate materials based on the ages, abilities, needs, and desired learning of participants in various settings.

As we choose curriculum for our congregation, we remember our understanding of God's grace and the way it works throughout our lives. The journey of faith is a lifelong process. God's saving power is open to all of us, no matter how much or how little we know of scripture, doctrine, and tradition. We do not

On what basis does your congregation choose its curriculum material? Who makes this choice?

have to learn certain content by a certain age in order to be saved. Our learning takes place as we meet again and again the stories of faith, and those stories gain meaning from events in our own life that make us say, "Yes, that's me! I've had that experience too." We want children, youth, and adults to learn, not because they need certain knowledge in order to be saved, but because learning about God is a joy and leads us to a richer and fuller life.

Those who plan the whole curriculum and those who teach particular materials need to understand the importance of the Bible. They must be able to use the Bible as a basic resource for their teaching, have a growing knowledge of the Bible, and encourage learners to read and study the Bible.

If you take a survey in your congregation and ask how many Bibles members have in their homes, you will find that most have several. But if you ask how many read and study the Bible on a regular basis, the number will be much smaller. We must use the Bible if we want it to be an important influence on teachers and learners. As we plan the whole curriculum for our congregation, we ask what we are doing to encourage daily use and study of the Bible, and we help our teachers increase their biblical knowledge and understanding. Unfortunately, many potential teachers do not believe they know enough about the Bible to teach. We can remind them that learning scripture and linking scripture to life are lifelong tasks. We can also create places where teachers feel comfortable being in partnership with those they teach, learning alongside those they teach, gaining together biblical knowledge and understanding.

In our planning we also remember that it is important to know and to teach the beliefs of our own tradition. When we know these beliefs, we internalize them and they become the values by which we live and judge life. Christian faith is lived faith, so, while Christian education begins with the learning of a

How might your congregation benefit from a survey of its Christian education needs?

How does your church help teachers learn scripture? How does it help them link that learning to daily living? How do teachers help others make connections between scripture and daily living?

system of beliefs, it also goes beyond that to be lived out day-by-day in our interactions with others. "The fact is our children, our young people, our adults need not so much to hear the Christian life described again as to see it lived. Real Christian education has to be dramatic, not just auditory."[5]

A *third stage* in curriculum development happens with each class. Teachers and students use the curriculum materials, changing and adapting them to meet their needs for each session. They use what is relevant, adapt other parts, and add new materials because each teaching/learning situation is unique.

A part of this adaptation is necessary because we cannot teach scripture, doctrines, and tradition in isolation from the world, and our particular place in the world is unique. We live in the midst of conflicting values, complex global issues, and great disparity between the rich and the poor. Because of television, we may know the news of countries halfway around the world better than we know the news of our own community. Our moral decisions may not be supported by others in the community where we live. And neither children nor older adults are valued in our world. Through our whole curriculum, we are to intentionally help people look at all of these issues and make faith decisions that they can live out at home, at church, at school, and in the workplace.

Last, and most important, we constantly remember the critical combination of teacher and curriculum materials. If you ask people what they remember from Sunday school when they were children, most will name a teacher. They will not easily remember the materials they used, the crafts they made, and the activities they enjoyed.

High quality curriculum materials play a vital role in effective teaching. However, the best materials can be undermined by a teacher who does not know and care for the students in the class or who is uninformed and unprepared. Conversely, a caring, faith-filled teacher may be able to work around poor materials and make the class inviting and informing for those who learn. The greatest contribution to life and faith is made by informed, prepared, caring, and faith-filled teachers using quality curriculum resources. Therefore our planning for the whole curriculum involves providing a wide variety of settings, selecting the best and most appropriate materials, and calling forth and supporting the most effective teachers.

How do you discern the needs of your learners?

Through teachers, settings, materials, and learners, we seek to nurture and be nurtured in the faith so that we can

> know and experience God through Jesus Christ, claim and live God's promises, and grow and serve as Christian disciples.

John Shea tells us:

> When we reach our limits, when our ordered worlds collapse, when we cannot enact our moral ideals, when we are disenchanted, we often enter into the awareness of Mystery. We are inescapably related to this Mystery which is immanent and transcendent, which issues invitations we must respond to, which is ambiguous about its intentions, and which is real and important beyond all else.

> Our dwelling within Mystery is both menacing and promising, a relationship of exceeding darkness and undeserved light. In this situation with this awareness we do a distinctively human thing. We gather together and tell stories of God to calm our terror and hold our hope high.[6]

May we tell the story in many and varied ways. May we take up the story and tell it again and again to any who will listen. And may we always invite others to join in the telling from generation to generation.

[1]Duane E. Ewers, *Our Ministry of Teaching*, Unpublished Paper.

[2]Peter L. Benson and Carolyn H. Elkin, *Effective Christian Education: A National Study of Protestant Congregations, A Summary Report on Faith, Loyalty, and Congregational Life* (Search Institute, 122 W. Franklin Ave., Minneapolis, MN, 1990). Reproduced by permission.

[3]Charles R. Foster, *Teaching in the Community of Faith* (Nashville: Abingdon Press, 1982), p. 154.

[4]Maria Harris, *Fashion Me a People: Curriculum in the Church* (Louisville, KY: Westminster/John Knox Press, 1989), p. 39.

[5]J. C. Wynn, *Christian Education for Liberation* (Nashville: Abingdon, 1977), p. 80.

[6]John Shea, *Stories of God* (Chicago: The Thomas More Press, 1978), Cover. Reproduced by permission of The Thomas More Press.

 NOTES

Conclusion
Into the Twenty-First Century

The United Methodist Church needs local congregations who have a vision for teaching and learning that will take them into the twenty-first century with creativity and vitality.

Our experience and research is clear. Christian education is not working well in many congregations. We are organized for the results we are getting. If we want different results, we need to do things differently.

We have some clues about what to do differently from some local congregations where Christian education is effective. *Foundations* has attempted to provide some clues about what we need to do as we move into the next century.

♦ We see teaching as a fundamental ministry of the community of faith as well as a series of programs.

♦ We pay more attention to the processes related to the educational ministry even as we look at the content of teaching.

♦ We live out our vision for teaching and learning in local congregations, with annual conferences and general church agencies giving support and encouragement.

◆ We emphasize teaching and learning for the community of faith as much as we emphasize it for individuals.

◆ We understand teaching as transformation as well as transmission of the stories, language, and symbols of the faith.

◆ We take who we teach, how they learn, and where they learn as seriously as we take content.

◆ We seek teachers with a growing and maturing faith as eagerly as we seek quality curriculum resources.

◆ We encourage teachers to develop their faith as well as their skills.

◆ We create new and different settings for learning at the same time that we strengthen traditional church schools.

◆ We integrate Christian education into the total life of the congregation, as well as see it as a unique ministry of the congregation.

Foundations offers us a variety of educational possibilities, identifies new patterns and approaches, and encourages us to act. We respond by exploring new ways of helping people and communities grow and mature in their faith and faithfulness.

Draw your congregation's spiritual road map. What paths has your congregation been on? Where has it found nourishment for the journey? How do your congregation's pathways move into the twenty-first century?

NOTES